Racism

A guide on how to become Anti-Racist, Raise Anti-Racist Children, and combat racism in our communities.

Gladys Maxwell

Contents

INTRODUCTION

What is Racism?

Racism can be defined as a situation where a person or group of persons are treated differently (negatively) because of their race, culture or color of their skin. Such treatment can include excluding them or possibly denying them some service at a business or denying them from job opportunities. In the United Kingdom (U.K) it is a crime to discriminate against (treat differently) someone/people because of their race.

Racism thoughts, arises from and is often linked to policies that causes harmful social, economic, cultural, and political differences. One of the major reasons why racism continues is because most people cannot see as clearly how the mind and body politic gradually harbors racist ideas.

Now that the public is looking for new answers about how to end institutional racism in the wake of George Floyd's death, who died after an officer kneeled on his neck for almost 9 minutes, you should take a considerable time to go over this text and possibly educate others on why racism should not be condoled in our society. The steps we can all take toward confronting the racist ideas we've held and what's required of us to become antiracist instead has been outlined in this book. In it you will also learn how to talk about racism with your kids, while striving to raise anti-racist children and the possible ways we can combat racism in our society/community.

HOW TO BECOME ANTI-RACIST:

1)   First understand the definition of racist

The English dictionary definition of racism goes thus; "a belief that race is the primary determinant of human traits and capacities and that racial differences produce an inherent superiority of a particular race. Discussions on racism often suffer when the discussants can't define the meaning of the word. Very few people would acknowledge that the definition reflects their views but nonetheless consciously or unwittingly believe in or endorse racist ideas.

A Racist can be said to be "A person who is in full support of a racist policy through their actions or inaction or expressing a racist idea." This incisive definition will force the reader to hold him or herself accountable for their ideas and actions.

How do we then define an antiracist? He can be said to be "A person who supports an antiracist policy through his or her actions or one who is expressing an antiracist idea."

2)   **Stop saying "I'm not racist"**

Saying "I'm not racist" isn't enough and most times it's a self-serving sentiment. Most people continue to change the definition of what racist is, so that it wouldn't apply to them. If you happen to be a non-violent white nationalist, then you might view the Ku Klux Klan as racist. Then if you're a Democrat, one who thinks there's something culturally wrong with black people, then racists in your view might be people who are Republicans

So, when you reflexively define yourself as not a racist, or beyond racism's firm hold, you're making it difficult to see how your own thoughts, ideas, and actions could be actually racist. Besides, being antiracist actually means moving beyond the "I'm not racist" defense and instead accepting and consciously articulating antiracist views and beliefs.

For instance, if you're a white liberal who regards herself "not a racist" but you refuse to enroll your child to a local public school because the vast majority of students are African American, that choice actually reflects racist thoughts. An antiracist would take a different position, and that would be to at least consider enrolling your child and/or learning about the disparities and inequities affecting that school in order to fight them.

3)   **Identify racial inequities and disparities**

Racism produces racial inequalities and differences in every area of private and public life. This includes both employment, politics, criminal justice health care, education, income, and home ownership. In becoming an antiracist, you must learn about and identify inequalities and differences that gives a racial group, material advantages over people of other color(s).

The first thing an anti-racist does is to identify racial inequities and deal with them.

For example, when Social Security was created in 1935, it excluded domestic and agricultural workers, and majority of these workers were black. Though the Social Security Administration was denying that racial bias was not a factor in that decision, but the decision still meant that black workers had less opportunity for a number of decades to gather savings and wealth compared to white workers. Other policies that disproportionately provided "tax-funded wealth-building opportunities" to white Americans produced similar results for black Americans.

Take Note that the first thing an anti-racist does is to identify racial inequities.

So, a racist analysis would give poor or worse outcomes for black Americans to the group's behavior or characteristics. An antiracist analysis would rather make a clear difference that the problem is not the group, but the policies that put racial groups at an obvious disadvantage.

4) Confront the racist ideas you've held or continue to hold

Once you start noticing racial inequities, check whether your own views, beliefs, or vote patterns have justified racial inequality.

If you're the type of parent who wouldn't send a child to a school that is predominant with blacks, then consider how your choice will influence your views on discipline policies and charter schools, policy issues that are deeply intertwined with race and racism. What is your position when it comes to voting? Would you vote for school board or city council candidates that do not want to address educational differences or would you work against local advocates who are trying to increase educational equity? Are you aware that funding such policies can affect how resources are disbursed to schools and why those practices can cause racial disparities? However, most people believe that these realities do not seem connected to whether or not they're racist. But for someone who wants to be anti-racist, you cannot afford to stay ignorant about them, or decline to change the policies that bring about disparities.

You can actually hold racist ideas without knowing they're biased, while still embracing ideas that are antiracist. If you don't know whether your beliefs or views are that of a racist, then listen to frontline racial justice advocates, activists, and organizations that have listed out antiracist positions and policies. Allow that listening to stir deeper reflection about why you've believed in certain ideas.

5)   Your antiracism ideas needs to be intersectional

Racist ideas and policies can affect many different people within racial groups. For instance, a policy that creates inequality between white and Native American people also produce inequality between white men and Native American women. If a person believes that black men have superiority over black women, then I'm sure that person would not be able to see how some particular ideas and policies inappropriately affect black women in dangerous ways.

Due to the fact that race cuts across various aspects of people's identities, including their gender, their sexuality, and ethnicity, it is important to use an intersectional approach when being antiracist.

6)   Champion antiracist ideas and policies

In your pursuit to become antiracist you must take necessary actions. And one of these actions is—

giving support to organizations in your society/community that are fighting policies which create racial disparities. You can either become a volunteer for or provide funds for those organizations. It is also recommended that you get into a position of power to enable you change racist policies in any setting where they exist, whether at school, work, government, etc. The idea is to commit one's self to some form of action that can possibly change racist policies.

MAKE YOUR KIDS UNDERSTAND WHAT IT MEANS TO BE ANTI-RACIST?

What does it mean to be anti-racist and how can adults talk to children about race and racism?

As a result of the current happenings in America, a lot of parents now see the need to talk about racism with their kids. Some of these parents actually admit that they do not know how to. Should parents teach and train their children not to be racist or to be anti-racist?

A good way to ensure that everyone's committed to eradicating racism is by making it a priority in raising anti-racist children.

From observations, when parents wish for their kids not to be racist, they actually do not talk about "race" to their kids. They would neglect any conversation about race or avoid explaining the racial inequities and disparities in their community. The end result is that, typically, those kids are being taught and learning to be racist by society.

In contrast however, when you want to really raise children to be anti-racist, you'll deliberately motivate them to talk about race and racism. That way, you will be intentionally teaching them that all the racial groups are equals. You will also be showing them that, truly there are different colors and there are different cultures, but we should give all of them equal values.

As a parent, if you don't talk openly to your children about racism, they will go out into the world and the society will make them racist. I'm sure you would agree with that?

When parents don't talk openly to their kids about racism, they will go out into the world and society will make them racist. Do you agree with that?

I think that it's very vital for parents and for educators to intentionally prepare our young people for the world that they are inheriting and living in. Not to talk about it is a great disservice to all young people. So, it's not just black students who need to learn about their skin color and their history, but white students as well and also non-black people of color need to learn their country's history and talk openly about it.

So, How Can You Talk About Race with Your Kids?

It is how you bring up conversations about race knowing how to engage your children in it makes the total difference in how they will view and accept others.

You must intentionally engage your children in these conversations on equality and race. This is very important to their racial identity, to their inclusiveness of others, and their ability to get involved in genuine relationships with others.

Your identity and your child's identity determine to a large extent, how you can talk to the child about racism. White parents can focus on recognizing their privileges and what it means to be an ally. While Parents of color might focus on preparing their children on how to face discrimination while also fostering resilience and helping them to enjoy their childhood, even though they might be facing serious discriminatory acts.

Although the context of these racist conversations and a child's needs constantly changes, there are however, some basic principles that can help parents of all backgrounds approach this challenge with great confidence.

Below are some of the ways white parents can engage their children in impactful and meaningful conversations on racism.

1.   Start talking to kids about racism early on

It's important for you to know that children start recognizing race and also start developing their racial sensibilities at a very early age. This is in contrast to the common misconception that they do not understand cultural and social attitudes until they're much older.

Also, children of color are most likely to have discriminative encounters from adults even if they're young. Research has shown that adults act on mild or implicit beliefs about race when communicating with children. A recent little research showed that participants noticed a threat when observing the faces of 5-year-old black boys.

So, it is not a bad idea to start the conversation about racism as early as when your child is 5 years old. That can make all the difference in how children see the world and others. Don't see it as the duty of the society to teach your children about racism. It won't do any good when you try to shelter your children from the harsh reality of what racism is. Deliberately teach them about racism and bias.

You have to be developmentally appropriate in your approach to the issue of race. Put your focus on explaining the goodness in others to younger children under the age of 10 and begin to teach your child about the history and systemic legacy of racism when they become adolescents, and also ways to become involved in making changes.

For younger kids, observe how they express their views. Reactively and proactively address their responses. Reactive response is about being open and interested when it comes up, and proactive response is about speaking of differences in physical features during play or while consuming entertainment in positive and normalizing ways. Both can significantly impact the thoughts and discussions they have about race in the future."

For kids that are older, ask them questions to find out about what they know, what they're being exposed to, how they discuss justice, fairness, and what ideas they have to make a positive difference in the world."

If you are still bothered that starting in an early age is premature, then consider how we often read books to children that are confusing or inscrutable.

We still do not understand why there is a portrait of bears sitting on chairs in Goodnight, Moon or three singing pigs in Moo, Baa, La LaLa! -- but those are the mainstays of early childhood.

2.   Do it often.

Though it's important to start early for a child in whatever age that the parent may deem appropriate, it is important to also engage the child in dialogues about race regularly.

From studies, it has been observed that, children start recognizing race and developing their racial sensibilities at a very early age.

Our lives are filled with numerous opportunities to bring up discussions about racism, discrimination and privileges that people experience. These moments don't have to be traumatic ones, either.

If you happen to discuss race for the first time in the wake of an international or national event, then give consideration to the previous opportunities you missed to start a conversation on race. Take for example, when the Oscar nominations are announced and OscarsSoWhite begins to trend, observe the controversy with your child. Also, when Beyoncé releases a new music video that makes reference to police shootings and Hurricane Katrina, endeavor to watch it with your child and be ready to start a conversation on it. If you watch the Republican presidential candidate Donald Trump on T.V arguing that Mexican immigrants are "rapists," discuss the inaccuracy of his statements with your child (children).

What is expected of you is that—you should normalize the discussion about race and ethnicity and make it look like ordinary experience.

This is not an indication that parents or guardians should feel it's an obligation to discuss about every single trending topic, but rather consider your child's approach to this topic by laying the foundation for a dialogue that unfolds over years.

3.   **Focus on empowerment.**

Each time you dialogue about people's oppression, you should also talk about people's resistance to power."

A parent didn't want her children to inherit the same absurd context for how they understood race, so she chose to focus on giving them examples of people of color who were passionate advocates for themselves and others.

Also, white parents should focus on teaching their children how to be allies, and how to use their privileges to demand on equal rights for all.

This does not mean you should presume to know how someone wants to be defended. Rather, allow the people of color to take the lead role, while you should simply provide the much-needed assistance and backup on their terms.

4.   **Never stop learning.**

By talking to children about race, adults therefore put a demand on themselves to assess their own values.

This is inclusive of parents and caregivers whose dedication on racial inclusivity and equity—as they might be surprised at their own biases. However, if adults claim to be perfect, it becomes hard to recognize their short-comings. They should rather accept their short-comings and see it as inevitable and also having a feeling of discomfort, at least once in a while, as it is a vital part of the process.

Most parents feel an undue pressure to get it right, and this is because of two reasons— one is because they don't plan to have a routine discussion, secondly-they mistakenly think their children are too fragile than they are.

By practicing humility, white parents can understand their own short-comings and also their children's abilities and needs.

This is a lifelong commitment.

5.   Acknowledge that white privilege is real.

Note that it is very appropriate and vital for white parents to teach their children about the privileges that they have simply because they are born as a white person. It's an important step in bringing up anti-racist children. Now, white privilege is not an indication that a white person will not have challenges or problems, but rather, it should be seen as an inherent advantage that the person has without having to do anything except to have a white skin.

White privilege is given to all white people of all gender, age, socio-economic status, geographical location or acknowledgment.

6.   Don't pretend color doesn't exist.

Consider race as an important matter. Research has shown that children can start to identify the difference in races in as early as 3 months old and can differentiate others by race around the age of 6 and 8 years old. So, if a parent starts to teach his/her children not to see color, then the parent is actually teaching the child not to know the identity of others. If you do not see a person's race, then you are saying that you do not need to know that person for real.

7.   Answer questions about race honestly and factually.

Children exhibit a high level of inquisitiveness while growing up, this is their way of trying to understand and learn. And most time in this situation—parents in trying to avoid embarrassment and ridicule, would give their children negative messages about race. They will make them see race as something to fear, or something not to give attention to. This will lay a very strong foundation for the child on how they see race and skin tone.

What you should rather do is to answer questions about race calmly and with humility. For instance, if your child says, "Dad, that man's skin is dark, and ours is white, agree with the child and ask him/her a question like, "what's your opinion about that?" or "Why did you say that?"

Be ready to accommodate their thoughts and questions. And most importantly, reply with real information. While taking note of differences, it also aids to point out similarities; this will prevent differences from leading to division.

Do not be judgmental so that they can open up to you. Ensure you correct inaccurate information and stereotypes. If for example, your child makes a negative statement about a person with a different hair texture, you can reply like this— "Her hair is not ugly, sweetie, her hair is curly, just like yours, but her curls look different from yours. And she can make beautiful hairstyles and wear bows just like you. Just because it is different from yours, doesn't make it bad".

8.   Be a good role model.

Your children are always looking up to you for guidance and they comprehend things more than you might think. They look up to you for not only what you can provide for them and teach them, but they also look out for how you do or do not respond to dialogues that bothers on racism".

Intentionally lay a good example to your children to follow. Be mindful of the language you use around them. Sketch out different ways you and your family can support people who may be experiencing discrimination and racism. You can do this by volunteering, donating, or just simply showing support.

9.   Don't hide your emotions.

It's important to show your children that it is ALRIGHT to be aware of your emotions and to discuss about them. If you feel unhappy about the present state of events around racial injustice, talk about it. If you are feeling frustrated, or you are probably confused, just talk about it.

It's alright if you feel like you don't know all the answers, but that does not indicate that discussions shouldn't take place. We want to teach our children the importance of having difficult dialogues. You can start a conversation with your child by talking about how you feel about the nationwide protests.

10.   Know that it's OK to feel uncomfortable.

It can be a very traumatic experience for a Black person to always answer questions like "how are you doing", especially with the current happenings that

that has made racism a trending topic. So, by way of showing support to dismantle racism, follow up your question with— "I'm sorry, you don't have to respond, but I want to assure you that my actions henceforth will be to support the Black society and end racism."

Hearing the above alone, might make you uncomfortable, so also is carrying out researches and educating yourself on how to raise anti-racist children, as it might make you nervous too. Do not be scared to feel that way. Step out of your comfort zone. Yes, you will feel uncomfortable and awkward, but you will definitely grow and become better.

RACISM HARMS CHILDREN

Racism can harm children in real and fundamental ways. Not only will their health be harmed, but even their chances to have a good and successful life can be jeopardized.

This is a wake-up call for all parents. If they care about the health and future of all their children, then they must take realistic steps to end racism — and also to support those who are affected by it.

Racism can affect our actions when we structure opportunities for and assign value to people based on our interpretation of how they look. Biologically we are actually just one race, and we share 99.9% of our genes despite the differences in our skin color or what part of the world we come from. But from history we have devised ways to not only identify differences, but also oppress people because of them. It was because of Racism that colonization and slavery was made possible. Even though biologically, we are the same, people will still continue to look for differences and claim superiority. Though we have made some historical progress, but the beliefs and oppression that go along with racism still persist; it is just as the AAP describes it, a "socially transmitted disease."

Racism is truly a disease and its effects can lead to chronic stress for children.

Chronic stress leads to changes in hormones that cause inflammation in the body, (and inflammation triggers chronic disease). The stress that a mother experiences during pregnancy can greatly affect children even before they are born. Though there have been improvements in the health care system, there still exist racial disparities in infant mortality as well as low birth weight.

Now, more than ever, it is imperative to think about chronic stress for the children of immigrant families.

Most of them live in perpetual fear of being separated from their parents if they haven't been already.

The children raised in African American, Hispanic, and American Indian populations are more prone to live in homes with higher unemployment and lower incomes than white children. This is an indication that they are less likely to enjoy good nutrition, good housing, access to good health care, and access to good education. Such disadvantages will increase their risk of having health problems and of receiving less, and lower-quality, education.

Even when less-privileged children live in privileged areas, studies have shown that they are always treated differently by teachers. They are prone to be punished harshly for minor offences. They are less likely to be seen as needing special education, and the teachers may look down on their abilities. The truth is—when a teacher doesn't believe in you, there is less chance that you will believe in yourself.

The AAP gave a report that in the 2015–2016 school year, 88% of white students graduated from high school. While only 76% of African Americans, 72% of American Indians and 79% of Hispanics did the same. These observations are necessary not in terms of economic opportunity but also for health purpose: adults with a college degree live longer, healthier and have lesser rates of falling ill with diseases than those who did not finish from college.

Another place where racism is displayed is the juvenile justice system. Youth of color are more prone to be incarcerated. And incarceration brings a lot of health and emotional issues, both during and after. Being incarcerated forever definitely changes a person — and changes others view of them.

Discrimination extends beyond racism

The point to note is —it is not just the color of one's skin (race) that can lead to discrimination and all the problems that come along with it. Things like differences in sex, religion, sexual orientation, and immigration status, having a disability, can also lead to discrimination.

Be reminded that children get hurt every day by racism and discrimination. And the effects of racism are not only permanent but continue through generations. Thus, there is an urgent call to dismantle racism in our communities.

HOW TO HELP CHANGE THE COURSE ON RACISM AND DISCRIMINATION?

Dismantling racism and discrimination is definitely not easy and quick. But there are things we can quickly do to cushion the effects of racism, see below:

1.   Let us take a hard look at ourselves, take account of our beliefs and our biases, and work rigorously to change them.

2.   We need to think about and change our manner of talking about each other, as individuals and as a society.

3.   We must always speak up when we hear or see racism or discrimination being displayed in any form. We should empower ourselves and each other as it is an important way to begin.

4.   We must engage our children in conversations about racism, and nurture them on healthier ways to think about themselves and others.

5.   We must work hard to stop institutional racism.

6.   We should also work hand in hand with our schools to be sure that all children, no matter the color, have access to a good and supportive education.

7.   We also have to be sure that there are structures in place to not only help people who are poor or struggling, but to bring them out of poverty.

8.   We must ensure our laws truly protect all people, and not just some people.

All of this is about the future of our children — and our children are our future.

WAYS TO HELP COMBAT RACISM IN YOUR SOCIETY

If you or someone you happen to know is experiencing racism or any form of discrimination, you can get help to make this stop. Below are a few guidelines to help combat racism in your community:

1.   Always recognize and get to know your own privilege.

The first basic step to dismantling racial discrimination is learning to recognize and understand your own privilege. We can clearly see how racial privilege plays out across social, political, economic, and cultural environments. So checking your privilege and using same to dismantle systemic racism are two great ways to start this complex process.

But note that race is just one aspect of privilege. Other aspects include: religion, gender, sexuality, ability-status, socio-economic status, language, and citizenship status and these can all affect your level of privilege. So, to use the privileges that you have to collectively empower others, you first need to be aware of those privileges and acknowledge their implications.

2.   Don't take the abuse

No matter what nationality or race, everyone has a right to live happily and free from discrimination. If you feel someone's attitude towards you is being racist the main thing is to walk away, stay safe and talk to someone you can trust. No need to retaliate or respond.

In case you feel discriminated against unlawfully, maybe at work or by a business, you can find out your right and give a report at Citizens Advice.

If you are experiencing any racist acts from someone, the most important thing is your safety, so walk away. If you feel unsafe, stay close to groups of friends that you trust.

Keep in mind that you're not the one stirring up trouble and you've done nothing wrong.

3.   Keep Evidence

Ensure to keep a note or diary of what's been happening and save any texts, or messages as evidence to show others how racists acts is affecting you and what support you need. In case you take action, any evidence you can put together will help your case.

4.   Tell Someone

Communicate with your teachers, youth workers, friends and/or family about what's going on so as to get their help and support.

5.   Report it.

Report any racist incidents to Police. Visit your local police station, fill out an online form or call the number provided.

If you can't speak English, ask the police to provide you an interpreter-they must provide you with one.

Take Note: you don't have to be the race or culture that someone has assumed you are when they say or do something to you in order for it to be a hate crime or incident.

6.   Stay safe on line

Again, if you are experiencing abuse online report it by using the 'report abuse' button which is made available on most social media platforms. Ensure your privacy settings are secure, too. The UK Safer Internet Centre provides some resources and guides on how to make sure all your social media accounts is private and secure.

You can also block anyone who is harassing or bullying you online.

7.   Get others involved

Talking about racism alone is a major part of fighting it. You could embark on an Anti-Racist project or newsletter at your school/youth group or set up a discussion group to dialogue about important issues and what you can do to help.

8.   Never give up

You cannot eradicate racism all by yourself but can get others involved to play their part. Combating racism when you see it (without getting yourself harmed) and reporting the situation helps to show other people that racism is not good.

9.   Support others

You can help to support someone who is suffering from racist acts. You can help by simply asking if they're okay and making them know that what you saw was wrong. You can also help them to report the event if they want and even volunteer to be a witness. This is known as "Third Party Reporting".

You can also challenge racism when you see it being displayed by people, by simply disagreeing to it.

10.   Examine your own biases and consider where they may have originated

What type of messages did you receive while growing up as a kid, about people who have a different skin color? What was the racial and ethnic structure of your school, neighborhood, or religious community? Why is the structure set up that way? These experiences give birth to and strengthens bias, stereotypes, and prejudice, and can in turn lead to discrimination. By examining our own biases, it would help us work hard in ensuring equality for all.

11.   Validate the experiences and feelings of people of color

Supporting the experiences of other people and engaging in serious dialogues about race and injustice is a great way to end racism in our society. We shouldn't be scared to talk about oppression and discrimination for the fear of "getting it wrong". Take bold steps by researching on the effects of racism in our society. A good example is, by watching documentaries, such as *13th*, or read books like *Americanah* or *Hidden Figures*.

A good advocate learns about domestic violence by listening to survivors of domestic violence. Also, the best way to understand racial inequities is by simply listening to people of color.

12.   Challenge the "colorblind" theory

It is a very misleading theory that we are living in a "post-racial" society where people "don't see color." This type of "colorblind" theory actually contributes to racism.

Dr. Martin Luther King, Jr. stated his hope for living in a colorblind world, but he did not mean that we should ignore color or race. Racism can never be eliminated without first acknowledging race. By being "colorblind" we tend to ignore a significant part of our identity and we dismiss the real injustices that many people encounter as a result of race. We must recognize color in order to work efficiently together for equity and equality.

13.   Call out racist "jokes" or statements.

Show people that racist comments are not normal or healthy. If you are not comfortable to be confrontational, try to explain their thought process with simplicity by asking questions. Say, your joke is not well understood, could you please explain it? Or "You may be joking, but it is the fact when you say that type of thing." Don't get scared to involve in discussions with your loved ones, colleagues, and friends. Minor-aggressions, which can come in the form of racist jokes or statements, can stir up biases and prejudices. Be reminded that by not saying anything – or laughing along with the jokes– indicates that you agree.

14.   Find out how your company or school works to expand opportunities for people of color.

Racism can exist in a system, which can be called "systematic racism". This means that there are barriers in a system which could include—imbalanced flow of wealth, criminal justice bias, and education and housing discrimination. This will affect the well-being of people of color in the workplace or at school. For instance, the African American Policy Forum (AAPF) gave a report that in 2014, a 12-year-old girl was faced with criminal charges. She was also expelled from school, just because she wrote "hi" on a locker room wall. Their campaign then, #BlackGirlsMatter, focused on the issues of over-policed and less-protected Black girls in the education system. It is crucial for schools and companies to address these issues and promote equity, fairness and justice.

15. Be thoughtful with your finances.

Be careful with your wallet. Understand the practices of companies that you wish to or already invest in and the charities that you donate to. Make efforts to do little shopping, do local businesses and give your money back to the people living in the community. Your state or community may have a data base of the local, minority-owned businesses in your area.

16. Adopt an intersectional approach in all aspects of your life.

Be reminded that all types of oppression are inter-related. So, you cannot fight against one form of oppression and not fight against the others.

Most of those who survive from domestic violence are also faced with racism and other forms of oppression. So, we must acknowledge and support survivors of these unique experiences.

CONCLUSION

So, if we want to make the world a better place for everyone to live in, let us do so by eliminating any form of oppression, discrimination and racism acts from our immediate environment, for example, our communities. Let us endeavor to be open and truthful in talking about race to our children and also work hard to raise them up as Anti-Racist kids, as our children are the future. When we do this, then we can rest assured that everyone will live in peace and harmony with no fear of getting harmed.

www.ingramcontent.com/pod-product-compliance
Lightning Source LLC
Chambersburg PA
CBHW051422250726
48655CB00003B/1178